ELEGIES

ELEGIES

MURIEL RUKEYSER

Introduction by Jan Heller Levi and Christoph Keller

A NEW DIRECTIONS BOOK

Elegies was originally published by New Directions in a limited slipcase edition of three hundred copies in 1949.

Manufactured in the United States of America
New Directions Books are printed on acid-free paper
First published as a New Directions Paperbook (NDP1263) in 2013
Published simultaneously in Canada by Penguin Books Canada Limited

Library of Congress Cataloging-in-Publication Data
Rukeyser, Muriel, 1913–1980.
[Elegiae. Selections]
Elegies / Muriel Rukeyser ; Introduction by Jan Heller Levi and Christoph Keller—First American paperback edition.
pages cm.
"A New Directions Book."
ISBN 978-0-8112-2106-1 (pbk. : alk. paper)
I. Levi, Jan Heller. II. Keller, Christoph. III. Title.
PS3535.U4E4 2013
811'.54—dc23
                    2013022288

10 9 8 7 6 5 4 3 2 1

New Directions Books are published for James Laughlin
by New Directions Publishing Corporation
80 Eighth Avenue, New York 10011

FOR OTTO BOCH

CONTENTS

NOURISH BEGINNINGS

Ten Notes on Muriel Rukeyser's Elegies

i.

Written over a decade of war—the Spanish Civil War, World
War II, the beginnings of the cold war—Muriel Rukeyser's *Elegies* capture the spirit, the anguish, and the desperate hopes of
that daunting, world-changing time. The elegies, as they were
written, appeared in three of Rukeyser's collections: the first
five in *A Turning Wind* (1939), the next four in *Beast in View*
(1944), and the tenth and final elegy in *The Green Wave* (1948).
In 1949, under the discerning stewardship of James Laughlin,
New Directions was the first to bring them all together, in a
handsome limited edition hand-signed and numbered in the

poet's distinctive turquoise-blue ink. Now, more than half a century later, here they are again together, in all their power, the full sweep of their ambition and achievement. They are no less relevant in our era of permanent war.

These poems, though rooted in key events of the decade in which they were written, are not reportage, not agitprop, not antiwar sloganeering. Rather, they are a profound poetic meditation on the sources of violence and love in our lives, and mark out the intersections — Rukeyser called these "meeting-places" — where such conflicting desires create new possibilities. In a world of upheaval, when survival seems the only course, these are poems of transformation.

ii.

In the summer of 1936, the twenty-two-year-old author of a groundbreaking first book, *Theory of Flight,* was asked by the London cultural journal *Life and Letters To-day* to cover the People's Olympiad in Barcelona, the antifascist alternative to the official Olympics in Berlin. Just past the town of Moncada, fifteen miles from Barcelona, Muriel Rukeyser's train ground to a halt amid shooting. Instead of arriving for the opening of the peaceful games, she found herself thrown into the first fighting of the Spanish Civil War.

Also on the train was an earnest young man from Germany named Otto Boch, a carpenter by trade but also a runner, on his way to Barcelona to compete in the Olympiad. Surrounded by the cruel soundtrack of gunfire and sirens, as Franco set his forces against the people of Spain, these two young people became lovers. Together they witnessed the beginnings of the Fascist will to power in Europe, and they recognized that they must take action. Boch remained to fight for the Republican cause. Five days later, Rukeyser was evacuated with other refugees, and returned to New York, where she worked for the American Medical Bureau to Aid Spanish Democracy. Boch's letters to her ceased to arrive after 1938; still, she held out hope that he had not perished.

Rukeyser was later to call her five days in Spain a "stroke of insight," the moment when she understood creative responsibility. "Then I began to say what I believe," she wrote in her introduction to *The Life of Poetry*.

iii.

Rilke's famous *Duino Elegies*, also a cycle of ten poems, appeared in the U. S. in a new translation by Stephen Spender and J. B. Leishman in 1939. Rukeyser, who read German, was already deeply familiar with them—they were a key inspiration for her work.

Rilke began his elegies in 1912, two years before Gavrila Prinzip's bullet toppled the tenuous order of Europe, though they wouldn't be completed until a decade later. "Prinzip's year bore us," Rukeyser wrote of her generation in "Poem Out of Childhood," "see us turning at breast / quietly while the air throbs over Sarajevo." In Trieste, the cosmopolitan port city of the Austrian Empire near Duino Castle, where Rilke was staying, the last pre-dreadnought battleships were being constructed and christened for a war that was sure to come.

> *Who, if I cried, would hear me among the angelic*
> *orders?*
>
> *
>
> *Strange, not to go on wishing one's wishes. Strange,*
> *to see all that was once relation so loosely fluttering*
> *hither and thither in space.*
>
> Rilke, *First Elegy*

Rukeyser began her elegies in New York in 1939, still hoping for word from her beloved in Spain. Barcelona and Madrid had already fallen, and it was likely Boch had fallen, too. Then Russia and Germany signed the devastating pact that spelled doom for Europe. From the window of her parent's apartment, she could see the Navy's new aircraft carriers and destroyers being launched on the Hudson River. As she had gone down to that river many times in her youth, now she goes down to "Rotten Lake," as she titled her first elegy, to discover

> *what must be crossed and cut out of your heart,*
> *what must be stood beside and straightly seen.*

*

Dare it arrive, the day when weakness ends?
When the insistence is strong, the wish converted?
I prophesy the meeting by the water
             of these desires.

                              First Elegy. Rotten Lake

iv.

Meanings, Rukeyser held, were the first casualties of war; the
search for meanings would always be deferred till "afterward,"
when it was too late, and the meanings were lost. The *Elegies*
do not wait.

v.

To see, without sentimentality, without self-pity, but with full
self-knowledge—that is the goal of these elegies, as it was the
goal of Rilke's: to imagine a way of being, a new unity. Living
in "the scraps of an age whose choice is seen / to lie between
evils," Rukeyser imagines a new kind of action:

   New combinations set out materials now,
   combine them again!   the existence is the test.
                          *

> *A man is walking, wearing the world, swearing*
> *saying You damn fools come out into the open.*
> *Whose dislocated wish? Whose terrors whine?*
> *I'll fuse him straight.*
> *The useable present starts my calendar.*
>
> > *Third Elegy. The Fear of Form*

vi.

Rukeyser has been called "difficult," she has been called "vague." Louise Bogan, never a friend to Rukeyser, called the *Elegies* "incoherent." But in demanding that creation, and the process of creation, be made visible on the page, Rukeyser is a pioneer of at least two generative practices in American poetry. In her perceptive early study *The Poetic Vision of Muriel Rukeyser* (1980), Louise Kertesz points out that Rukeyser anticipated Charles Olson and Robert Duncan's proposals of the poem as a field of energy. Rukeyser writes in *The Life of Poetry* in 1949:

> *Exchange is creation.*
> *In poetry, the exchange is one of energy. Human energy is transferred, and from the poem it reaches the reader. Human energy, which is consciousness, the capacity to produce change in existing conditions.*

And this is Olson a year later in his essay "Projective Verse":

> *A poem is energy transferred from where the poet got*
> *it ... by way of the poem itself, all the way over, to*
> *the reader ... the poem itself must, at all points, be*
> *a high energy-construct, and at all points, an energy-*
> *discharge.... And it involves a whole series of new*
> *recognitions.*

Moreover, in the *Elegies*, Rukeyser continues and extends her fractal amplifications of micro and macro, of the American landscape and the American character, first explored in her documentary modernist classic "Book of the Dead." In the "Fifth Elegy. A Turning Wind," Rukeyser brings to the page what we now recognize as a radical ecopoetics. The poem is an ideal, if complex, expression of her famous quote from 1972: "It isn't that one brings life together—it's that one will not allow it to be torn apart."

vii.

An unfolding exploration of the meeting-places between contradictory desires—welcome frictions and expansions creating new definitions of peace: let's ask ourselves why the *Elegies* (not to mention Rukeyser's "Letter to the Front") do not appear in recent anthologies of World War II poetry, such as *Poets of World War II* (Library of America, 2004), *American War Poetry* (Columbia University Press, 2006) or *The Poetry of War* (Cambridge University Press, 2008).

As Rukeyser would ask, What resource are we not using?

viii.

"You've achieved a kind of tragic optimism that most of us are still trying to define," the poet and critic John Malcolm Brinnin wrote to her.

ix.

> *Nourish beginnings, let us nourish beginnings.*
> *Not all things are blest, but the*
> *seeds of all things are blest.*
> *The blessing is in the seed.*
>
> > *Tenth Elegy. Elegy in Joy*

Rukeyser's son William Laurie had just been born when she wrote her last elegy.

"Nourish beginnings," something women tend to be good at. And being a woman, being a mother, being busy breast-feeding and writing about it, she walked, or was walked, stroller-pushing, out of the carefully sentried canon. Maybe it is this way she became, in Anne Sexton's words, "the mother of us all."

x.

Otto Boch lost his life in battle at the Ebro River on April 11, 1938. Rukeyser received confirmation more than five years later, on Christmas Eve 1943, from Ernst Toller. "He was cut down, with 300 out of 700," Rukeyser noted in her journal that evening. She continues: "I still love what I have always loved ... I believe in faith and resistance. Not: faith, meaning belief in that which is *against* natural processes, but an extension, the conclusion to which the *images* lead me." In 1949, she dedicated the *Elegies* to Otto Boch.

JAN HELLER LEVI
& CHRISTOPH KELLER
MAY 2013

ELEGIES

First Elegy

ROTTEN LAKE

As I went down to Rotten Lake I remembered
the wrecked season, haunted by plans of salvage,
snow, the closed door, footsteps and resurrections,
        machinery of sorrow.

The warm grass gave to the feet and the stilltide water
was floor of evening and magnetic light and
reflection of wish, the black-haired beast with my eyes
        walking beside me.

The green and yellow lights, the street of water standing
point to the image of that house whose destruction
I weep when I weep you.   My door (no), poems, rest,
    (don't say it!) untamable need.

*

When you have left the river you are a little way
nearer the lake; but I leave many times.
Parents parried my past; the present was poverty,
the future depended on my unfinished spirit.
There were no misgivings because there was no choice,
only regret for waste, and the wild knowledge :
growth and sorrow and discovery.

When you have left the river you proceed alone;
all love is likely to be illicit; and few
friends to command the soul; they are too feeble.
Rejecting the subtle and contemplative minds
as being too thin in the bone; and the gross thighs
and unevocative hands fail also.   But the poet
and his wife, those who say Survive, remain;
and those two who were with me on the ship
leading me to the sum of the years, in Spain.

When you have left the river you will hear the war.
In the mountains, with tourists, in the insanest groves
the sound of kill, the precious face of peace.

And the sad frightened child, continual minor,
returns, nearer whole circle, O and nearer
all that was loved, the lake, the naked river,
what must be crossed and cut out of your heart,
what must be stood beside and straightly seen.

*

As I went down to Rotten Lake I remembered
how the one crime is need.   The man lifting the loaf
with hunger as motive can offer no alibi, is
             always condemned.

These are the lines at the employment bureau
and the tense students at their examinations;
needing makes clumsy and robs them of their wish,
             in one fast gesture

plants on them failure of the imagination;
and lovers who lower their bodies into the chair
gently and sternly as if the flesh had been wounded,
             never can conquer.

Their need is too great, their vulnerable bodies
rigidly joined will snap, turn love away,
fear parts them, they lose their hands and voices, never
             get used to the world.

Walking at night, they are asked Are you your best friend's
best friend? and must say No, not yet, they are
love's vulnerable, and they go down to Rotten Lake
            hoping for wonders.

Dare it arrive, the day when weakness ends?
When the insistence is strong, the wish converted?
I prophesy the meeting by the water
            of these desires.

I know what this is, I have known the waking
when every night ended in one cliff-dream
of faces drowned beneath the porous rock
            brushed by the sea;

suffered the change : deprived erotic dreams
of images of that small house where peace
walked room to room and always with one face
            telling her stories,

and needed that, past loss, past fever, and the
attractive enemy who in my bed
touches all night the body of my sleep,
            improves my summer

with madness, impossible loss, and the dead music
of altered promise, a room torn up by the roots,
the desert that crosses from the door to the wall,
       continual bleeding,

and all the time that will which cancels enmity,
seeks its own Easter, arrives at the water-barrier;
must face it now, biting the lakeside ground;
       looks for its double,

the twin that must be met again, changeling need,
blazing in color somewhere, flying yellow
into the forest with its lucid edict :
       take to the world,

this is the honor of your flesh, the offering
of strangers, the faces of cities, honor of all your wish.
Immortal undoing! I say in my own voice. These prophecies
       may all come true,

out of the beaten season. I look in Rotten Lake,
wait for the flame reflection, seeing only
the free beast flickering black along my side
       animal of my need,

and cry I want! I want! rising among the world
to gain my converted wish, the amazing desire
that keeps me alive, though the face be still, be still,
the slow dilated heart know nothing but lack,
now I begin again the private rising,
the ride to survival of that consuming bird
beating, up from dead lakes, ascents of fire.

Second Elegy

AGE OF MAGICIANS

A baroque night advances in its clouds,
maps strain loose and are lost, the flash-flood breaks,
the lifting moonflare lights this field a moment,
while death as a skier curves along the snows,
death as an acrobat swings year to year,
turns down to us the big lace of a nurse.
Roads open black, and the magicians come.

The aim of magicians is inward pleasure.
The prophet lives by faith and not by sight,
Being a visionary, he is divided,

9

or Cain, forever shaken by his crime.
Magnetic ecstasy, a trance of doom
mean the magician, worshipping a darkness
with gongs and lurid guns, the colors of force.
He is against the unity of light.

The Magician has his symbols, brings up his children by them :
the march-step, the staircase at night, the long cannon.
The children grow in authority and become
Molitor, Dr. Passavant, powerful Dr. Falcon,
bring their professors, and soon may govern
the zone, the zodiac, the king on his throne.
"Because the age holds its own dangers.
Because snow comes with lightnings, omens with all seasons."
(The Prophet covers his face against the wall,
weeps, fights to think again, to plan to start
the dragon, the ecliptic, and the heart.)

The Magician lifts himself higher than the world.
The Prophets were more casual.   They endured,
and in the passive dread of solitude
heard calls, followed veiled, in midnight humility.

They claimed no preference; they separated
unity from blindness
living from burning
tribute from tribute.

They have gone under, and do they come again?
The index of prophecy is light
and steeped therein
the world with all its signatures visible.

*

Does this life permit its living to wear strength?
Who gives it, protects it.   It is food.
Who refuses it, it eats in time as food.
It is the world and it eats the world.
Who knows this, knows.   This has been said.
This is the vision in the age of magicians :
it stands at immense barriers, before mountains :
'I came to you in the form of a line of men,
and when you threw down the paper, and when you sat at the play,
and when you killed the spider, and when you saw the shadow
of the fast plane skim fast over your lover's face.
And when you saw the table of diplomats,
the newsreel of ministers, the paycut slip,
the crushed child's head, clean steel, factories,
the chessmen on the marble of the floor,
each flag a country, each chessman a live man,
one side advancing southward to the pit,
one side advancing northward to the lake,
and when you saw the tree, half bright half burning.
You never enquired into these meanings.
If you had done this, you would have been restored.'

The word is war.
And there is a prediction that you are the avenger.

They cut the people's hands, and their shoulders were left,
they cut their feet off, and their thighs were whole,
they cut them down to the torse, but the voice shouted,
they cut the head off, but the heart rang out.

And in the residential districts, where nothing ever happens,
armies of magicians filled the streets,
shouting
Need! Bread! Blood! Death!

And all this is because of you.
And all this is avenged by you.
Your index light, your voice the voice,
your tree half green and half burning,
half dead half bright,
your cairns, your beacons, your tree in green and flames,
unbending smoke in the sky, planes, noise, the darkness,
magic to fight. Much to restore, now know. Now be
Seer son of Sight, Hearer, of Ear, at last.

Third Elegy

THE FEAR OF FORM

Tyranny of method! the outrageous smile
seals the museums, pours a mob skidding
up to the formal staircase, stopped, mouths open.
And do they stare? They do.
At what? A sunset?

Blackness, obscurity, bravado were the three colors;
wit-play, movement, and wartime the three moments;
formal groups, fire, facility, the three hounds.

This was their art : a wall daubed like a face,
a penis or finger dipped in a red pigment.

13

The sentimental frown gave them their praise,
prized the wry color, the twisted definition,
and said, "You are right to copy."
But the car full of Communists put out hands and guns,
blew 1 - 2 - 3 on the horn before the
surrealist house, a spiral in Cataluña.

New combinations set out materials now,
combine them again! the existence is the test.
What do you want? Lincoln blacking his lessons
in charcoal on an Indiana shovel?
or the dilettante, the impresario's beautiful skull
choosing the tulip crimson satin, the yellow satin
as the ballet dances its tenth time to the mirror?
Or the general's nephew, epaulets from birth,
run down the concourse, shouting Planes for Spain?

New methods, the staring circle given again
force, a phoenix of power, another Ancient
sits in his circle, while the plaster model
of an equation slowly rotates beneath him,
and all his golden compass leans.

Create an anti-sentimental : Sing!
"For children's art is not an asylum art,
there are these formal plays in living, for
the equal triangle does not spell youth,
the cube nor age, the sphere nor ever soul.

Asylum art is never children's art.
They cut the bones down, but the line remained.
They cut the line for good, and reached the point
blazing at the bottom of its night."

*

A man is walking, wearing the world, swearing
saying You damn fools come out into the open.
Whose dislocated wish?   Whose terrors whine?
I'll fuse him straight.
The useable present starts my calendar.
Chorus of bootblacks, printers, collectors of shit.
Your witwork works, your artwork shatters, die.
Hammer up your abstractions.   Divide, O zoo.
—He's a queer bird, a hero, a kangaroo.
What is he going to do?

He calls Rise out of cities, you memorable ghosts
scraps of an age whose choice is seen
to lie between evils.   Dazzle-paint the rest,
it burns my eyes with its acetylene.
Look through the wounds, mystic and human fly,
you spiritual unicorn, you clew of eyes.

Ghosts to approach the blood in fifteen cities.
Did you walk through the walls of the Comtesse de Noailles?
Was there a horror in Chicago?
Or ocean?   Or ditches at the road.   Or France,

while bearing guarding shadowing painting in Paris,
Picasso like an ass Picasso like a dragon Picasso like a
romantic movement
and immediately after, stations of swastikas
Prague and a thousand boys swing circles clean
girls by the thousand curl their arms together
geometries of wire
the barbed, starred
Heil

Will you have capitals with their tarnished countesses
their varnished cemetery life
vanished Picassos
or clean acceptable Copenhagen
or by God a pure high monument
white yellow and red
up against Minnesota?

Does the sea permit its dead to wear jewels?
Flame, fusion, defiance are your three guards,
the sphere, the circle, the cluster your three guides,

Adam, Godfinger, only these contacts function :
light and the high accompanied design,
contact of points the fusion say of sex
the atombuster too along these laws.
Put in a sphere, here, at the focal joint,

he said, put it in. The moment is arrangement.
Currents washed through it, spun, blew white,
fused. For! the sphere! proving!

This was the nightmare of a room alone,
the posture of grave figure, finger on other head,
he puts the finger of power on him,
optic of grandiose illusion.
All you adjacent and contagious points,
make room for fusion; fall,
you monuments, snow on your heads,
your power, your pockets, your dead parts.

Standing at midnight corners under corner-lamps
we wear the coat and the shadow of the coat.
The mind sailing over a scene lets light arrive
conspicuous sunrise, the knotted smoke rising,
the world with all its signatures visible.
Play of materials in balance,
carrying the strain of a new process.
Of the white root, the nature of the base,
contacts, making an index.
And do they stare? They do.
Our needs, our violences.
At what? Contortion of body and spirit.
To fuse it straight.

Fourth Elegy

THE REFUGEES

And the child sitting alone planning her hope :
I want to write for my race.   But what race will you speak,
being American?   I want to write for the living.
But the young grow more around us every day.
They show new faces, they come from far, they live
occupied with escape, freeze in the passes, sail
early in the morning.   A few arrive to help.
           Mother, those were not angels, they were knights.

Many are cast out, become artists at rejection.
They saw the chute, the intelligible world

so wild become, it fell, a hairy apparent star
this time with not a public saint in sight
to record miracle. The age of the masked and the alone begins,
we look for sinister states, a loss shall learning suffer
before this circle of this sun be done,
the palace birds of the new tyrants rise
flying into the wounded sky, sky of catastrophe;
help may be near, but remedy is far,
rain, blood, milk, famine, iron, and epidemic
pour in the sky where a comet drags his tail.
The characters of the spectacles are dead,
nothing is left but ventriloquists and children,
and bodies without souls are not a sacrifice.

It is the children's voyage must be done
before the refugees come home again.
They run like lemmings out
building their suffocated bodies up
to let the full stream pass.
The predatory birds sail over them.
They dash themselves into lighthouses, where the great lights
                                        hold up,
they laugh at sympathy : "Have you nothing better to do in the
                                        trenches?"

And at that brink, that bending over doom,
become superior to themselves, in crisis.
There is an addition and fusion of qualities.

They are the children.   They have their games.
They make a circle on a map of time,
skipping they entered it, laughing lifted the agate.
I will get you an orange cat and a pig called Tangerine.
The gladness bird beats wings against an opaque glass.
There is a white bird in the top of the tree.
They leave their games, and pass.

Cut.   Frozen and cut.   Off at the ankle.   Off at the hip.
    Off at the knee.   Cut off.
Crossing the mountains many died of cold.

We have spoken of guilt to you too long.
The blame grows on us who carry you the news.
And as the man bringing the story of suicide
lives with the fact, feels murder in himself,
as murderous regents with their gentle kings
know the seductions of crime long before death takes hold,
we bear their—

     a child crying shrill in a white street
"Aviación!" among the dust of geysers,
the curling rust of Spanish tile.
We bear their smile, we smile under the guilt,
in an access of sickness, "Let me alone, I'm healthy!"
cry.   And in danger, the sexually witty
speak in short sentences, the unfulfilled.
While definition levels others out.

Wish : the unreality of fulfilled action.
Wish : the reality of fulfilled thought.
Images of luxury.   Image of life.
A phoenix at play among the peonies.
The random torture predicts the random thought.
Over the thought and bird and flowers, the plane.

Coming to strange countries refugee children find
land burned over by winter, a white field and black star
falling like firework where no rockets are
into hell-cities with blank brick and church-bells
(I like this city.   This is a peaceful city)
ringing the bees in the hot garden with their mixing sounds,
ringing the love that falters among these hills,
red-flowering maple and the laugh of peace.
It will take a bell-ringing god tremendous imagined descending
for the healing of hell.

A line of birds, a line of gods.   Of bells.
And all the birds have settled on their shadows.
And down the shadowed street a line of children.
You can make out the child ahead of you.
It turns with a gesture that asks for a soft answer.
It sees the smaller child ahead of it.
The child ahead of it turns.   Now, in the close-up
faces throw shadow off.   It is yourself
walks down this street at five-year intervals,

seeing yourself diminishing ahead,
five years younger, and five years younger, and young,
until the farthest infant has a face
ready to grow into any child in the world.

> They take to boats.   The shipwreck of New York.
> To trains whose sets of lines pass along boxes,
> children's constructions.
> Rush to rejection
> foreknowing the steps,
>> disfigurement of women, insults of disease,
>> negations of power.   They people the earth.
>> They are the strong.   They see the enemy.
>> They dream the relaxed heart, coming again to power,
>> the struggle, the Milk-Tree of Children's Paradise.

They are the real creation of a fictional character.
They fuse a dead world straight.

A line of shadowy children issues, surf issues it,
sickness boiled in their flesh, but they are whole,
insular strength surrounds them, hunger feeds them strong,
the ripened sun finds them, they are the first of the world,
free of the ferryman Nostalgia, who stares at the backward shore.
Growing free of the old in their slow growth of death,
they hold the flaming apples of the spring.
They are exposed to danger.

Ledges of water trick them,
they fall through the raw colors of excavations,
are crushed by monuments, high stone like whale-blow rising,
the backwash of machines can strike them down.
A hill on a map claims them, their procession reaches
a wavy typographical circle where
two gunners lie behind their steelwork margins,
spray shot across the line, do random death
They fire in a world infected by trenches,
through epidemics of injuries, Madrid, Shanghai,
Vienna, Barcelona, all cities of contagion,
issue survivors from the surf of the age.
Free to be very hungry and very lonely.
And in the countries of the mind, Cut off at the knee.   Cut off
                at the armpit.   Cut off at the throat.
Free to reclaim the world and sow a legend,
to make the adjustments never made,
repair the promises broken and the promise kept.
They blame our lives, lie on our wishes with their eyes our own,
to say and to remember and avenge. A lullaby for a believing child.

Fifth Elegy

A TURNING WIND

Knowing the shape of the country. Knowing the midway travels of
migrant fanatics, living that life, up with the dawn and
moving as long as the light lasts, and when the sun is falling
            to wait, still standing;

and when the black has come, at last lie down, too tired to
turn to each other, feeling only the land's demand under them.
Shape that exists not as permanent quality, but varies with
            even the movement of bone.

Even in skeletons, it depends on the choices of action.
A definite plan is visible.   We are either free-moving or
fixed to some ground.   The shape has no meaning
                    outside of the function.

Fixed to Europe, the distant, adjacent, we lived, with the land-
promise of life of our own.   Course down the East—frontiers
meet you at every turn—the headlights find them, the plain's,
                    and the solar cities

recurrent centers.   And in the middle of the great world the wind
answers the shape of the country, a turning traveller
follows the hinge-line of coast, the first indefinite
                    axis of symmetry

torn off from sympathy with the past and planted,
a primitive streak prefiguring the west, an ideal
which had to be modified for stability,
                    to make it work.

Architecture is fixed not only by present needs but
also by ancestors.   The actual structure means a plan determined
by the nature of ancestors; its details are determined by
                    function and interference.

There are these major divisions : for those attached to the sea-floor,
a fan at freedom, flexible, wavering, designed to catch food
from all directions. For the sedentary, for those who crouch and look,
        radial symmetry,

spokes to all margins for support. For those who want movement,
this is achieved through bilateral symmetry only,
a spine and straight attack, all muscles working,
        up and alive.

                              *

And there are years of roads, and centuries of need,
of walking along the shadow of a wall, of visiting houses,
hearing the birds trapped in the wall, the framework trembling
        with struggles of birds,

years of nightwalking in stranger cities, relost and unnamed,
recurrent familiar rooms, furnished only with nightmare,
recurrent loves, the glass eye of unreal ambition,
        years of initiation,

of dishallucination on the diamond meadows,
seeing the distances of false capes ahead,
feeling the tide-following and turning wind,
        travelling farther

under abrasive weather, to the bronzy river,
the rust, the brown, the terrible dead swamps,
the hanging moss the color of all the hanged,
            cities whose heels

ring out their news of hell upon all streets,
churches where you betray yourself, pray ended desire,
white wooden houses of village squares. Always one gesture :
            rejecting of backdrops.

These are the ritual years, whose lore is names of shapes,
Grabtown, Cockade Alley, Skid Row where jobless live,
their emblem a hitch-hiker with lips basted together,
            and marvel rivers,

the flooded James, a double rainbow standing over Richmond,
the remnant sky above the Cape Fear River, blue stain on red water,
the Waccamaw with its bone-trees, Piscataqua' s rich mouth,
            red Sound and flesh of sand.

—A nation of refugees that will not learn its name;
still shows these mothers enduring, their hidden faces,
the cry of the hurt child at a high night-window,
            hand-to-hand warfare,

the young sitting in libraries at their only rest
or making love in the hallway under an orange bulb,
the boy playing baseball at Hungry Mother State Park,
   bestiaries of cities

and this shape, this meaning that promises seasonal joy.
Whose form is unquietness and yet the seeker of rest,
whose travelling hunger has range enough, its root
   grips through the world.

The austere fire-world of night : Gary or Bethlehem,
in sacred stalks of flame—or stainless morning,
anti-sunlight of lakes' reflections, matchlight on face,
   the thorny light of fireworks

lighting a way for the shape, this country of celebrations
deep in a passage of rebirth. Adventures of countries,
adventures of travellers, visions, or Christ's adventures
   forever following him

lit by the night-light of history, persevering
into the incredible washed morning air.
The luisarne swamp is our guide and the glare ice,
   the glow of tracklights,

the lights winding themselves into a single beacon,
big whooping riders of night, a wind that whirls
all of our motives into a single stroke,
        shows us a country

of which the birds know mountains that we have not dreamed,
climbing those unsuspected slopes they fade. Butte and pavilion
vanish into a larger scape, morning vaults all those hills
        rising on ranges

that stand gigantic on the roots of the world,
where points expand in pleasure of raw sweeping
gestures of joy, whose winds sweep down like stairs,
        and the felled forests

on hurricane ridges show a second growth. The dances
of turkeys near storm, a pouring light, tornado
umbilical to earth, fountains of rain, a development
        controlled by centers,

until the organs of this anatomy are fleshed away at last
of gross, and determining self, develop a final structure
in isolation. Masterpieces of happiness arrive,
        alive again in another land,

remembering pain, faces of suffering, but they know growth,
go through the world, hunger and rest desiring life.
Mountains are spines to their conquest, these wrecked houses
        (vines spiral the pillars)

are leaning their splintered sides on tornadoes, lifted careening
in wheels, in whirlwind, in a spool of power
drawing a spiral on the sun, drawing a sign of
        strength on the mountains,

the fusing stars lighting initiated cities.
The thin poor whiteness raining on the ground
forgotten in fickle eclipses, thunderbirds of dream
        following omens,

following charts of the moving constellations.
Charts of the country of all visions, imperishable
stars of our old dream : process, which having neither
        sorrow nor joy

remains as promise, the embryo in the fire.
The tilted cities of America, fields of metal,
the seamless wheatfields, the current of cities running
        below our wings

promise that knowledge of systems which may bless.
May permit knowledge of self, a lover's wish of conversion
until the time when the dead lake rises in light,
the shape is organised in travelling space,
this hope of travel, to find the place again,
rest in the triumph of the reconceived,
lie down again together face to face.

Sixth Elegy

RIVER ELEGY

In burning summer I saw a season of betrayal,
the world fell away, and wasteful climbing green
covered the breaking of bodies, covered our hearts.
Unreal in the burning, many-motioned life
lay like a sea, but fevers found my grief.
I turned in that year to retrieve the stainless river,
the lost, the flowing line of escaped music.

Year of judgement!   Century of betrayal!
They built their cities on the banks of war
and all their cities are down, the Floating Man
swims in the smoke of their sky, the Double Woman

smiles up through the water with her distorted mouth.
I stand over reflection as the world darkens in
destruction of countries, all souls downward set,
life narrowing to one color of a choked river
and hell on both its banks.   My city, my city!
They never built cities.   Cities are for the living.
They built for the half-dead and the half-alive.
Their history is a half-history.   And we go down.
They built their villages whose lame towers fell
where error was overgrown until the long
tentacular ruin touches all fields.   My love!
Did I in that country build you villages?
Great joy my love, even there, until they fell
and green betrayal climbed over the wall.

Defeat and raging and a burning river.
Half-faced, half-sexed, the living dead arrive
passing, a lip, a breast, half of a hand.
Gaudy sadistic streets, dishonest avenues
where every face has bargained for its eyes.
And they come down to the river, driven down.
And all the faces fly out of my city.
The rich streets full of empty coats parading
and one adolescent protesting violin,
the slums full of their flayed and faceless bodies,
they shiver, they are working to buy their skin.
They are lost.   They come down to look for life in a river,
plunge, turn and plunge, they cannot change their life,
swimming, their head is in another world.

World without form.   Chaos beaten and beaten,
raging and suffering and hoping to take shape.
I saw your summer.   I saw your river flow.
I being wasted everywhere saw waste.
Hell's entropy at work and torment general,
friend against most-known friend, love fighting off love.
They asked for an end to emptiness; their sick throats filled with foam,
prayed to be solved, and rose to deal betrayal.
And I falling through hell passed many friends, and love,
and a haunted woman warned me as I fell.
Downward through currents, the horrors with little hands.

The chaos, the web of the heart, this bleeding knot;
raises me swimming now, one moment in the air
and light is on my face, the fans over the river
of wind, of goodness.   Lie gasping on this shore,
there is nothing in the world but an honest word
which the severed away may speak before we die.
Let me tell you what I have held to all along :
when I said that I loved you, when I crossed the frontier,
when I learned the obscurities of a frightened child,
when I shut the door, and felt the sprouting tears,
when I saw the river, when I learned resurrection,
the joy of your hands in a pain that called More Life.
Let me tell you what I have meant all along :
meaning of poetry and personal love,
a world of peace and freedom, man's need recognised,
and all the agonies that will begin that world.

Betrayed, we are betrayed.   The set of the great faces
mean it, the following eyes.   They are the flayed men,
their strength is at the centre, love and the time's disease
lie at their skin.   The kiss in the flaring garden
when all the trees closed in.   The knotted terrible lips.
The black blood risen and the animal rage.
The last fierce accident, whose back-thrown drowning head
among the escaping sound of water hears
slow insane music groping for a theme.

My love, reach me again.   The smell of the sea,
wind-flower, sea-flower, the fallen gull-feather.
Clear water and order and an end to dreams :
ether-dreams, surrounded beasts, the aftertoll of fear,
the world reduced to a rising line of water,
the patient deserted by the analyst.
To keep the knowledge that holds my race alive :
spiritual grace of the material world.

I walked under the sky, and the high clouds
hollowed in ribs arched over their living heart :
the world, the corporeal world that will not die.
No, world's no heart—here is yourself walking
in a cage of clouds looking up wanting one face
over you and that look to fill the sky.
Carrying counter-agony into the world,
dream-singing, river-madness, the tragic fugal love
of a theme balancing another theme.

Disorder of suffering, a flight of details, a world
with no shadows at noontime and never at night a light.
Suddenly the flame-blue of a drunken sky
and it is the change, the reds and metals of autumn.
But I curse autumn, for I do not change,
I love, I love, and we are far from peace,
and the great river moves unbearably;
actual gestures of giving, and I may not give.
Water will hold my shadows, the kiss of darkness,
maternal death's tender and delicate promises
seethe at the lips, release and the full sleep.

Even now the bright corporeal hand
might come to redeem the long moment of dying.
Even now if I could rest my life,
my forehead on those knees and the arriving shadows
in rising quiet as the long night arrives.
Terror, war, terror, black blood and wasted love.
The most terrible country, in the heads of men.
This is the war imagination made;
it must be strong enough to make a peace.
My peace is strong enough if it will come
flowing, the color of eyes. When the world burns away
nothing is left can ever be betrayed.

All broken promises, adulterate release—
cast in the river of Death, charred surface of waste,
a downward soulset, never the old heaven

held for a moment as breath held underwater;
but we must rise into a breathing world.
And this dark bellowing century, on its knees—?
If all this must go down, it must.
And all this brilliance go to dust?
Only the meanings can remain alive.
When the cemeteries are military objectives
and love's a downward drawing at the heart
and every letter bears the stamp of death.

There is no solution.   There is no happiness.
Only the range must be taken, a way be found to use
the inmost frenzy and the outer doom.
They are here, they run their riot in the clouds,
fly in our blood and over all our mountains,
corrupt all waters, poison the pride of theme.

Years of judgement!   Century screaming for
the flowing, the life, the intellectual leap
of waters over a world grown old and wild,
a broken crying for seasonal change until
O God my love in time the waste become
the sure magnificent music of the defeated heart.

Seventh Elegy

DREAM-SINGING ELEGY

Darkness, giving us dream's black unity.
Images in procession start to flow
among the river-currents down the years of judgement
and past the cities to another world.

There are flat places. After the waterfall
arched like the torso of love, after the voices
singing behind the waterfall, after the water
lying like a lover on the heart,
there is defeat.

And moving through our spirit in the night
memories of these places.
Not ritual, not nostalgia, but our cries,
the axe at the heart, continual rebirth,
        the crying of our raw desire,
        young. O many-memoried America!

                *

In defeat there are no prophets and no magicians,
only the look in the loved and tortured eyes
when every fantasy restores, and day denies.
The act of war debased to the act of treason
in an age of treason. We were strong at the first.
We resisted. We did not plan enough. We killed.
But the enemy came like thunder in the wood,
a storm over the treetops like a horse's head
reared to a great galloping, and war
trampled us down. We lost our young men in the fighting,
we lost our homeland, our crops went under the frost,
our children under the hunger. Now we stand
around this fire, our black hills far behind,
black water far before us, a glitter of time on the sea,
glitter of fire on our faces, the still faces—
stillness waiting for dreams
and only the shadows moving,
shadows and revelations.

In the spring of the year, this new fighting broke out.
No, when the fields were blond.   No, the leaves crimson.
When the old fighting was over, we knew what we were
seeing as if for the first time our dark hills masked with green,
our blond hills with the trees flame-shaped and black
in burning darkness on the unconsumed.
Seeing for the first time the body of our love,
our wish and our love for each other.
Then word came from a runner, a stranger :
"They are dancing to bring the dead back, in the mountains."
We danced at an autumn fire, we danced the old hate and change,
the coming again of our leaders.   But they did not come.
Our singers lifted their arms, and a singer cried,
"You must sing like me and believe, or be turned to rock!"

The winter dawned, but the dead did not come back.
News came on the frost, "The dead are on the march!"
We danced in prison to a winter music,
many we loved began to dream of the dead.
They made no promises, we never dreamed a threat.
And the dreams spread.
But there were no armies, and the dead were dead,
there was only ourselves, the strong and symbol self
dreaming among defeat, our torture and our flesh.
We made the most private image and religion,
stripped to the last resistance of the wish,
remembering the fighting and the lava beds,

the ground that opened, the red wounds opening,
remembering the triumph in the night,
the big triumph and the little triumph—
wide singing and the battle-flash—
assassination and whisper.

In the summer, dreaming was common to all of us,
the drumbeat hope, the bursting heart of wish,
music to bind us as the visions streamed
and midnight brightened to belief.
In the morning we told our dreams.
They all were the same dream.

Dreamers wake in the night and sing their songs.
In the flame-brilliant midnight, promises
arrive, singing to each of us with tongues of flame :
We are hopes, you should have hoped us,
we are dreams, you should have dreamed us."
Calling our name.

When we began to fight, we sang hatred and death.
The new songs say, "Soon all people on earth
will live together." We resist and bless
and we begin to travel from defeat.
Now, as you sing your dream, you ask the dancers,
in the night, in the still night, in the night,
"Do you believe what I say?"
And all the dancers answer "Yes."

To the farthest west, the sea and the striped country
and deep in the camps among the wounded cities
half-world over, the waking dreams of night
outrange the horrors.   Past fierce and tossing skies
the rare desires shine in constellation.
I hear your cries, you little voices of children
swaying wild, nightlost, in black fields calling.
I hear you as the seething dreams arrive
over the sea and past the flaming mountains.
Now the great human dream as great as birth or death,
only that we are not given to remember birth,
only that we are not given to hand down death,
this we hand down and remember.

Brothers in dream, naked-standing friend
rising over the night, crying aloud,
beaten and beaten and rising from defeat,
crying as we cry : We are the world together.
Here is the place in hope, on time's hillside,
where hope, in one's image, wavers for the last time
and moves out of one's body up the slope.
That place in love, where one's self, as the body of love,
moves out of the old lifetime towards the beloved.
Singing.

Who looks at the many colors of the world
knowing the peace of the spaces and the eyes of love,
who resists beyond suffering, travels beyond dream,

knowing the promise of the night-flowering worlds
sees in a clear day love and child and brother
living, resisting, and the world one world
dreaming together.

Eighth Elegy

CHILDREN'S ELEGY

Yes, I have seen their eyes.   In peaceful gardens
the dark flowers now are always children's eyes,
full-colored, haunted as evening under fires
showered from the sky of a burning country.

Shallow-featured children under trees
look up among green shadows of the leaves.
The angel, flaming, gives—into his hands
all is given and he does not change.
The child changes and takes.
All is given.   He makes and changes.
The angel stands.

45

A flame over the tree.   Night calling in the cloud.
And shadow among winds.   Where does the darkness lie?

It comes out of the person, says the child.
A shadow tied and alive, trying to be.

In the tremendous child-world, everything is high,
active and fiery, sun-cats run through the walls,
the tree blows overhead like a green joy,
and cloudy leopards go hunting in the sky.

The shadow in us sings, "Stand out of the light!"
But I live, I live, I travel in the sun.

*

On burning voyages of war they go.
Like starving ghosts they stumble after nuns.
Children of heroes, Defeat the dark companion.
But if they are told they are happy, they will know.

Who kills the father burns up the children's tears.
Some suffering blazes beyond all human touch,
some sounds of suffering cry, far out of reach.
These children bring to us their mother's fears.

Singing, "O make us strong O let us go—"
The new world comes among the old one's harms,

old world carrying new world in her arms.
But if they say they are free, then they will know.

War means to me, sings a small skeleton,
only the separation,
mother no good and gone,
taken away in lines of fire and foam.
The end of war
will bring me, bring me home.

The children of the defeated, sparrow-poor and starved,
create, create, must make their world again.
Dead games and false salutes must be their grace.
One wish must move us, flicker from our lives
to the marred face.

My child, my victim, my wish this moment come!
But the martyr-face cries to us fiercely
"I search to learn the way out of childhood;
I need to fight.   I wish for home."

That is what they say, who were broken off from love :
However long we were loved, it was not long enough.

We were afraid of the broad big policeman,
of lions and tigers, the dark hall and the moon.

After our father went, nothing was ever the same,
when mother did not come back, we made up a war-game.

My cat was sitting in the doorway when the planes
went over, and my cat saw mother cry;
furry tears, fire fell, wall went down;
did my cat see mother die?

Mother is gone away, my cat sits here coughing.
I cough and sit. I am nobody's nothing.

However long they loved us, it was not long enough.
For we have to be strong, to know what they did, and then
our people are saved in time, our houses built again.

You will not know, you have a sister and brother;
my doll is not my child, my doll is my mother.

However strong we are, it is not strong enough.
I want to grow up.   To come back to love.

*

I see it pass before me in parade,
my entire life as a procession of images.
The toy, the golden kernel, the glass lamp.
The present she gave me, the first page I read,
the little animal, the shadowless tall angel.

The angel stands.   The child changes and takes.
He makes a world, stands up among the cousins,
cries to the family, "Ladies and gentlemen—
The world is falling *down!*" After the smooth hair
darkens, and summer lengthens the smooth cheek,
and the diffuse gestures are no longer weak,
he begins to be the new one, to have what happened,
to do what must be done.

O, when the clouds and the blue horse of childhood
melt away and the golden weapons,
and we remember the first public day's
drums and parades and the first angel
standing in the garden, his dark lips
and silver blood, how he stood,
giving, for all he was was given.

I begin to have what happened to me.

O, when the music of carousels and stars
is known, and the music of the scene
makes a clear meeting, greeting and claim of gods,
we see through the hanging curtain of the year
they change each other with one change of love!
See, in one breath, in a look!
See, in pure midnight a flare of broken color
clears to a constellation.

Peace is asleep, war's lost. It is love.
I wanted to die. The masked and the alone
seemed the whole world, and all the gods at war,
and all the people dead and depraved. Today
the constellation and the music! Love.

You who seeking yourself arrive at these lines,
look once, and you see the world,
look twice, and you see your self.

And all the children moving in their change.

To have what has happened, the pattern and the shock;
and all of them walk out of their childhood,
give to you one blue look.

And all the children bowing in their game,
saying Farewell, Goodbye; Goodbye, Farewell.

Ninth Elegy

THE ANTAGONISTS

Pieces of animals, pieces of all my friends
prepare assassinations while I sleep.
They shape my being, a gallery of lives
fighting within me, and all unreconciled.
Before them move my waking dreams, and ways
of the spirit, and simple action.   Among these
I can be well and holy.   Torn by them I am wild,
smile and revenge myself upon my friends
and find myself among my enemies.
But all these forms of incompleteness pass
out of their broken power to a place
where dream and dream meet and resolve in grace.

The closing of this conflict is the end
of the initiation.   I have known the cliff
and known the cliff-dream of the faces drowned.
Stood in the high sun, a dark girl looking down,
seeing the colors of water swaying beneath me, dense
in the flood-summer, various as my love
and like my hope enchanted.   Drawn to blue
chance and horizons, and back as sea-grasses move
drawn landward slowly by incoming tides—
and then the final cancelling and choice,
not tilted as flowers under wind, but deep
blessing of root and heart, underwater swung,
wrenched, swayed, and given fully to the sea.
Heaven not of rest, but of intensity.

The forms of incompleteness in our land
pass from the eastern and western mountains where
the seas meet the dark islands, where the light
glitters white series on the snowlands, pours its wine
of lenient evening to the center.   Green
on shadows of Indiana, level yellow miles ...

The prairie emblems and the slopes of the sky
and desert stars enlarging in the frost
redeem us like our love and will not die.
All origins are here, and in this range
the changing spirit can make itself again,
continually love, continually change.

Out of the myth the mother leaned;
From out the mother shines the child;
Man rises, in the mass contained;
And from this growth creation grows.
The fire through all the spiral flows :
Create the creative, many-born!
And use your love, unreconciled!

*

In wheels, in whirlwind, in a storm of power
alive again and over every land
the thunderbird with lightnings at his wrists.

Eclipses uncloud and show us miracle,
gleaming, our ancestors, all antagonists :
Slave and Conquistador, dead hand-to-hand,
scented fastidious Tory with his whore,
distinguished rebel and woman at the plow.
The fiery embryo umbilical
always to failure, and form developing
American out of conflict.

Fierce dissenting ghosts,
the second Adam's fever and eagle voice
and Jackson's muscular and democratic sense.
Sprung in one birth John Brown, a mad old man
whose blood in a single broken gesture freed
many beliefs, and Lincoln's agony

condemning and confirming. O, they cry,
the oppositions cry, O fight for me!
Fight, you are bound to freedom, and be free!
When Hawthorne saw the fabulous gift, he tore
flesh from his guilt, and found more guilt; the bells
rang barter of the self, but Melville drowned.
The troubled phantoms bring to our terrible
chaos the order of a meeting-place
where the exchange is made, the agonies
lie down at last together face to face.

In the black night of blood, the forms begin
to glitter alive, fathers of constellations,
the shining and the music moving on.
We are bound by the deepest feuds to unity.
To make the connections and be born again,
create the creative, that will love the world.

*

Not glistening Indies, not continents, but the world
opening now, and the greatness of our age
that makes its own antagonists of the wish.
We want to find and will spend our lives in finding :
the landfall of our broken voyages
is still our America of contradictions.
Ancestors of that dream lie coupled in our flesh,
pieces of animals, pieces of all our friends
meet in us and we live. We do not die.

Magical keen Magellan sought a rose
among the compass and legendary winds.
Green sequels rocked his eyes in water; he
hung with the scorpion sun on noon's glass wall,
stared down, down into the future as he sailed.
Fanatic travels, recurrent mysteries.
Those who want the far shore spend their lives on the ocean.
The hand of God flowers in coasts for these.

Those who want only home spend their lives in the sky.
Flying over tonight, while thirteen searchlights join
high incandescent asters on black air.
The blinding center fastens on a plane
floating and white, glare-white; he wanting land
and intimate fertile hours, hangs there.   Sails
great scends of danger, or wades through crazy sand.

Those who most long for peace now pour their lives on war.
Our conflicts carry creation and its guilt,
these years' great arms are full of death and flowers.
A world is to be fought for, sung, and built;
Love must imagine the world.

                    The wish of love
moving upon the body of love describes
closing of conflict, repeats the sacred ways
in which the spirit dances and survives.

To that far meeting-place call home the enemies —
they keep their oppositions, for the strong
ironic joy of old intensities
still carries virile music.

                    O, the young
will come up
          after us
             and make the dream
the real world of our myth.
                  But now, the song
they will discover is a shadowy theme —

Today we are bound, for freedom binds us — we
live out the conflict of our time, until
Love, finding all the antagonists in the dance,
moved by its moods and given to its grace,
resolves the doom
              and the deliverance.

Tenth Elegy

ELEGY IN JOY

Now green, now burning, I make a way for peace.
After the green and long beyond my lake,
among those fields of people, on these illuminated
hills, gold, burnt gold, spilled gold and shadowed blue,
the light of enormous flame, the flowing light of the sea,
where all the lights and nights are reconciled.
The sea at last, where all the waters lead.
And all the wars to this peace.

For the sea does not lie like the death you imagine;
this sea is the real sea, here it is.

58

This is the living.   This peace is the face of the world,
a fierce angel who in one lifetime lives
fighting a lifetime, dying as we all die,
becoming forever, the continual god.

Years of our time, this heart!   The binding of the alone,
bells of all loneliness, binding our lands and our music,
branches full of motion each opening its own flower,
lands of all song, each speaking in his own voice.
Praise in every grace
among the old same war.

Years of betrayal, million death breeding its weaknesses
and hope, buried more deep more black than dream.
Every elegy is the present—freedom eating our
hearts, death and explosion, and the world unbegun.
Now burning and unbegun, I sing earth with its war,
and God the future, and the wish of man.

*

Though you die, your war lives : the years fought it,
fusing a dead world straight.

The living will be giving you your meanings,
widening to love because of the love of man.
All the wounds crying
I feare, and hope : I burne, and frese like yse ...
saying to the beloved

For your sake I love cities,
on your love I love the many,
saying to the people,
for your sake I love the world.
The old wounds crying
I find no peace, and all my warres are done.

> Out of our life the living eyes
> See peace in our own image made,
> Able to give only what we can give :
> Bearing two days like midnight. "Live",
> The moment offers; the night requires
> Promise effort love and praise.

Now there are no maps and no magicians.
No prophets but the young prophet, the sense of the world.
The gift of our time, the world to be discovered.
All the continents giving off their several lights,
the one sea, and the air.   And all things glow.
Move as this sea moves, as water, as force.
Peace shines from its life, its war can become
at any moment the fierce shining of peace,
and all the life-night long many voices are saying
The name of all things is Glowing.

A beginning, a moment of rest that imagines.
And again I go wandering far and alone,
I rise at night, I start up in the silence—

lovely and silver-black the night remembers.
In the cities of America I make my peace;
among the bombs and commands,
the sound that war makes
NO   NO
We see their weeping and their life-time dreams.
All this, they say to us, because of you.
Much to begin.   Now be your green, your burning,
bear also our joy, come to our meeting-place
and in the triumph of the reconceived
lie down at last together face to face.

*

We tell beginnings : for the flesh and the answer,
for the look, the lake in the eye that knows,
for the despair that flows down in widest rivers,
cloud of home; and also the green tree of grace,
all in the leaf, in the love that gives us ourselves.

The word of nourishment passes through the women,
soldiers and orchards rooted in constellations,
white towers, eyes of children :
saying in time of war What shall we feed?
I cannot say the end.

Nourish beginnings, let us nourish beginnings.
Not all things are blest, but the
seeds of all things are blest.
The blessing is in the seed

This moment, this seed, this wave of the sea, this look, this instant
                                   of love.
Years over wars and an imagining of peace. Or the expiation journey
toward peace which is many wishes flaming together,
fierce pure life, the many-living home.
Love that gives us ourselves, in the world known to all
new techniques for the healing of the wound,
and the unknown world.   One life, or the faring stars.